THE
IRON GOAT
TRAIL

THE
IRON GOAT
TRAIL

A Guidebook

Second Edition

**Becky Wandell for
Volunteers for Outdoor Washington**

**THE
MOUNTAINEERS**

Published by
The Mountaineers
1001 SW Klickitat Way, Suite 201
Seattle, WA 98134

Volunteers for Outdoor Washington

© 1999 by Volunteers for Outdoor Washington
The Mountaineers Books in cooperation with
Volunteers for Outdoor Washington

First edition, 1993; second edition, 1999

Published simultaneously in Great Britain by Cordee
3a DeMontfort Street, Leicester, England, LE1 7HD

Manufactured in the United States of America

Edited by Paula Thurman
Maps by Jerry Painter
Illustrations by James A. Engelhardt
Cover and book design by Kristy L. Welch
Layout by Peggy Egerdahl
Cover photograph: *The Martin Creek Crossover* © Ruth Ittner
Frontispiece: *Great Northern locomotive No. 1964 in front of the east portal of First
Cascade Tunnel. (Photo: James Turner, Warren W. Wing collection)*

Library of Congress Cataloging-in-Publication Data

Wandell, Becky
    The Iron Goat Trail : a guidebook / Becky Wandell for Volunteers
for Outdoor Washington ; [edited by Paula Thurman]. – 2nd ed.
        p.   cm.
    "The Mountaineers Books in cooperation with Volunteers for Outdoor
Washington"-T.p. verso.
    Includes bibliographical references.
    ISBN 0-89886-624-3
    1. Hiking–Washington (State)–Iron Goat Trail–Guidebooks.
2. Iron Goat Trail (Wash.)–Guidebooks. 3. Great Northern Railway
Company (U.S.)–History. I. Thurman, Paula. II. Volunteers for
Outdoor Washington. III. Title.
    GV199.42.W22I769 1998
917.97'50443–dc21   98-50805
                                                           CIP

Contents

FOREWORD AND ACKNOWLEDGMENTS

The first edition of *The Iron Goat Trail: A Guidebook* was developed by the USDA Forest Service (USFS), with Volunteers for Outdoor Washington (VOW) as part of the team. Published in time for the dedication of the Martin Creek segment of the trail in October 1993, it interpreted only that portion. The second edition has been revised and expanded to include the Wellington segment. It has been developed by VOW, with Becky Wandell, the interpretive specialist who prepared the Wellington Interpretive Plan, as the author and the Forest Service as part of the team. Support for Ms Wandell's work on the guidebook as well as on the trail's interpretive signs was provided by the King County Landmarks and Heritage Commission Hotel-Motel Tax Fund.

Over the years that VOW and the USFS have worked in partnership to construct, maintain, and interpret the Iron Goat Trail, many people became involved in the project and were eager to contribute their knowledge of the Great Northern (GN) Railway's fascinating history to this revised edition. The result was a much larger manuscript than originally planned. Fortunately, Emily Horswill, an award-winning writer with thirty years of experience, was available to rigorously edit the text down to a more manageable size without losing the story.

Marion Langstaff ably coordinated and facilitated the entire manuscript review process. On the review team, Jim Mattson, a retired GN employee who organized GN documents for the Museum of History and Industry (Seattle), provided detailed information on the GN's infrastructure. Robert Kelly's research focus and collection of photos on Wellington gave an in-depth dimension to the story. Art Benedict and Al Hunter, railroad buffs and civil engineers, provided an overall perspective and a sense of direction. Mike Sharpe, as representative of the Great Northern Railway Historical

Society, and Larry Lynde, with his very special collection of photos, made valuable contributions. Ruth Munson prepared the plant list and Evelyn Peaslee the bird list for the Appendixes. Skykomish Ranger District personnel who were helpful in the review process include retired Cultural Resource Assistant Glenn Katzenburger, Trails Specialist Tom Davis, and Public Services Manager Jerry Zimmerman. Dr. Grant Sharpe, Professor Emeritus of Interpretation, College of Forest Resources, University of Washington, advised on interpretive themes and trail signage. Sam Fry meticulously checked facts and figures. Kim Forman, former Public Affairs Officer for the Great Northern Railway, reviewed the manuscript, as did Charles Intlekofer, a retired Great Northern Chief Engineer. Willie Jones, historian and electrical engineer for Burlington Northern Santa Fe, and David L. Huelsbeck, Associate Professor of Anthropology, Pacific Lutheran University, were helpful in answering specific questions. Martin Burwash, author of the book *Cascade Division*, reviewed the manuscript.

My heartfelt thanks to all who so generously contributed to the development of this book. We all hope that this guidebook will enrich your experience along the trail.

Ruth Ittner
Iron Goat Trail Coordinator

The trail is named "Iron Goat" because the Rocky Mountain goat was featured in the Great Northern Railway's logo.

 # THE TRAIL'S BEGINNING

The Iron Goat Trail is located on the upper and lower sections of an abandoned Great Northern Railway grade. You can walk this route today thanks to the vision of Volunteers for Outdoor Washington (VOW) and the USDA Forest Service. In 1987 they joined forces and, with the cooperation of others, turned the idea for a trail into reality. The trail provides access to a National Historic Civil Engineering Landmark and the Stevens Pass Historic District.

Years before trail construction began, VOW built support for the project, compiled historical information, and evaluated the trail's environmental consequences by identifying the unique plants and birds found along its way. Volunteers bushwhacked possible trail locations and created an access route through the fallen timber and avalanche debris that had accumulated over sixty years.

In 1992 trail construction began with volunteers involved in all areas of the project: coordination and planning, survey and design, construction, archaeological digs, historical research, and interpretation.

Thanks to the teamwork of volunteers, organizations, and government agencies, the initial 4 miles of trail were dedicated on October 2, 1993—one hundred years after the first Great Northern Railway train crossed the Cascades.

Volunteer work parties continued and as of October 1998, 1,200 volunteers have dedicated 50,400 hours to this trail. By the end of 1999, 8 miles of trail and two different trailheads will be open for hiking. The dedication for this section of trail will be held in the year of 2000—one hundred years after the opening of the first Cascade Tunnel. Volunteers for Outdoor Washington and the U.S. Forest Service would like to thank all who made this trail possible.

Volunteers clearing the route for the Iron Goat Trail. (Photo: Ruth Ittner)

Plans are underway for a third access point. The barrier-free trail along the lower grade will be extended from the Martin Creek Trailhead to the historic townsite of Scenic on U.S. Highway 2. Volunteer work parties will continue in order to achieve this goal.

GETTING THERE

The Iron Goat Trail can be accessed from two trailheads, one at Martin Creek and the other at Wellington. Universally accessible toilets are available at both trailheads.

To reach the **Martin Creek Trailhead** from the **Puget Sound area:**
- Drive east on U.S. Highway 2 to Milepost 55, which is 6 miles beyond the town of Skykomish.
- Turn left onto the Old Cascade Highway (USFS Road 67).
- Proceed 2.3 miles to the highway's junction with USFS Road 6710.
- Turn left and proceed 1.4 miles to the trailhead parking lot.

From **Wenatchee** and **points east:**
- Drive west over Stevens Pass on U.S. Highway 2 to Milepost 58.4 at Scenic, which is 5.5 miles west of the summit of Stevens Pass.
- Turn right on the Old Cascade Highway (USFS Road 67).
- Proceed 1.4 miles to the highway's junction with USFS Road 6710.
- Turn right and proceed 1.4 miles to the trailhead parking lot.

To reach the **Wellington Trailhead:**
- Drive U.S. Highway 2 to Milepost 64.4 just west of Stevens Pass and turn north on the Old Stevens Pass Highway. (If you are coming from the Puget Sound area, because of limited sight distance you should proceed east to Stevens Pass, turn around at the crest of the hill where visibility is optimum, and return to Milepost 64.4.)
- Proceed 2.8 miles on the Old Stevens Pass Highway to its junction with USFS Road 050.
- Turn right and proceed to the trailhead parking lot.

ABOUT THE TRAIL

The Iron Goat Trail follows the original route of the railroad and is divided into two levels (see map on pages 36-37). The Lower Grade can be accessed from the Martin Creek Trailhead and is linked with the Upper Grade via two short, steep trails referred to as the Martin Creek and Corea Crossovers. The wide, nearly level Lower Grade has a barrier-free, compacted surface suitable for wheelchairs and the physically challenged and goes downhill from the Martin Creek Trailhead at a 2.2 percent grade. Currently 1.2 miles of the Lower Grade are open to hikers, with 1.5 more miles expected to be added soon after the year 2000.

The Upper Grade can be accessed from both trailheads and is open to hiking for 6 miles. If you are starting at the Martin Creek Trailhead, there will be a short but steep ascent from the Lower Grade to the Upper Grade via the Martin Creek Crossover, then a gradual uphill hike at a 2.2 percent grade to Wellington. The hike along the Upper Grade from Wellington to Martin Creek is downhill at the same grade.

Using the Trail

This trail is a day-use site for hikers and the physically challenged. A Trail Park Pass is required to park at the trailheads. Passes can be purchased at the USFS ranger station 1 mile east of Skykomish or at other ranger stations. The U.S. Forest Service uses the funds from these passes for trail and trailhead maintenance.

Please help us ensure that your visit is safe and that the area is preserved for generations to come:

- Pick up litter, but leave flowers, rocks, and historic artifacts in place so that others may continue to enjoy them.
- Stay on the trail, out of tunnels, and off old timbers, which are prone to collapse.
- Please respect private property. The trail right-of-way is on USFS land and is located within the Stevens Pass Historic District. Some surrounding areas include private property.
- The trail is neither maintained nor patrolled during the winter when many avalanche chutes are active. If you plan to visit the trail in winter, be prepared and check avalanche conditions by calling the Avalanche Forecast Center at (206) 526-6677.

# The Trail's History

As you walk the Iron Goat Trail, listen for the rumbling of trains passing through the valley below. The trains operate on a track that belongs to the Burlington Northern Santa Fe Railway—a direct descendant of the Great Northern Railway. But for thirty-six years around the turn of the last century, the grade beneath your feet was part of Great Northern's line.

Here, hundreds of immigrants labored to clear the hills of giant trees, drill and blast rock to create a flat grade, and establish camps for the hundreds of workers needed to maintain the tracks. Harsh winters made it difficult and expensive to keep the line open, and in 1929, after the completion of a new 7.8-mile-long tunnel in the valley below, the Great Northern Railway abandoned this section. The camps were torn down, people moved elsewhere, and thick vegetation reclaimed this mountainside.

The story of the Great Northern Railway is a story of vision, ambition, perseverance, and sweat. It is largely the story of James J. Hill, a shrewd man known as the Empire Builder, and of the thousands of people who toiled to make his vision a reality.

THE EMPIRE BUILDER

Born in a small town in Canada, James J. Hill arrrived in St. Paul, Minnesota, in 1856, at the height of the riverboat era. Adventurers looking for fortunes in gold and timber were pushing the frontier westward and Hill foresaw that railroads would replace riverboats and horse-drawn wagons, linking the country to northwest ports for overseas trade. With this in mind, Hill joined with others to buy the

One harsh winter, a Great Northern Railway engine plows its way through four and one-half feet of wet, settled snow. (Photo: University of Washington Libraries, Special Collections, Pickett 3034A)

bankrupt St. Paul and Pacific Railroad and subsequently formed the Great Northern Railway in 1889, with a vision of building a railroad that would reach the Pacific Coast.

By 1887 the rival Northern Pacific Railroad had crossed the Cascades at Stampede Pass, linking Tacoma with points east. Hill, however, saw Seattle as the ideal terminus for a northern route and began his extension west in 1890, one year after Washington became a state.

CROSSING THE MOUNTAIN WILDERNESS

The rugged Cascades posed a serious problem for the railway. John F. Stevens, an engineer for the Great Northern, had earlier found an easy route over the Rocky Mountains and was assigned to do the same in the Cascades. Stevens soon located a low pass over the Cascade crest, which his assistant, Charles F. B. Haskell, identified by carving the name "Stevens Pass" in a nearby tree.

Hill ordered his engineers to build "the shortest and best line," but crossing the steep Cascades proved to be a difficult task. The most direct way to cross Stevens Pass was to tunnel through solid granite. But Hill could not justify this enormous cost and postponed initial plans to construct a tunnel. Instead, engineers designed a series of switchbacks, three on the east side and five on the west side of the Cascade crest. Twelve miles of track connected Cascade Station on the east side of Stevens Pass with Wellington on the west (the two points were just 3 miles apart as the crow flies).

Finally, in the cold of winter, the railroad reached the Pacific Coast. The first ceremonial train arrived in Seattle on January 8, 1893. Regular scheduled service between St. Paul and Seattle started on June 18, 1893.

A LABORIOUS JOURNEY

Crossing the Cascades was a daily challenge. Trains heading east from Skykomish stopped at Scenic for coal and water before grinding around a sharp curve to head west toward Corea. Soon the trains crossed a long timber trestle over Martin Creek, labored through the Horseshoe Tunnel, where they curved around almost 180 degrees, and emerged traveling east again over another trestle. Two more miles brought them to Embro for a water stop, and then, still climbing the 2.2 percent grade, they struggled

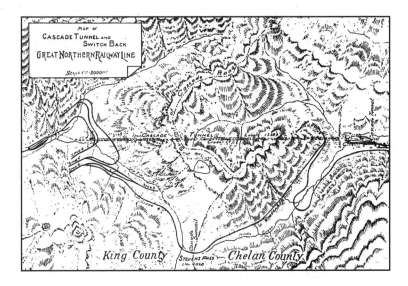

To get trains over Stevens Pass, engineers designed a series of eight switchbacks, three on the east side and five on the west. The troublesome switchbacks were later replaced by a 2.6-mile-long shortcut tunneled through solid granite.

around Windy Point, 650 feet above the town of Scenic. After taking on more coal and water at Wellington, trains ascended the 4 percent-grade switchbacks on the western slopes of Stevens Pass.

Two engines in the front and one in the back pushed and pulled trains upward toward the summit. Passengers found themselves traveling forward and then backward as the train traveled up a switchback, then pulled onto a spur and stopped so that the engine at the opposite end of the train could become the lead for the next switchback. Allowing time for meeting other trains and being delayed by rock slides and so forth, a trip over the Cascades could take between five and twenty hours.

Imagine those winter crossings over the mountains with snow piled as high as 25 feet on either side of the tracks, creating an icy canyon that muffled sound. Sometimes snowslides trapped trains for days at a time until snowplows and hundreds of laborers could shovel the way clear.

Despite the difficult trip, the ride was usually smooth. Passengers received meal service in the dining car complete with elegant silver, china, glassware, and linens on the table. The early transcontinental trains—the Oriental Limited and the Empire Builder—had sleepers

CASCADE DIVISION.--Main Line. Leavenworth to Seattle.

	TRAINS GOING WEST.						TRAINS GOING EAST.	
	Time Freight No. 15 Daily	Passenger No. 3 Daily	Distance from East Spokane	STATIONS	Distance between Stations	Telegraph Calls	Passenger No. 4 Daily	Fre'ght No. 16 Daily
	lv 3 17am	lv 9 27am	204.4	Leavenworth	4.0	CH	ar 3 05pm	ar 10 54am
	4 33	9 59	212.0	Chiwaukum	10.6	CJ	2 32	{ 9 59 / 9 20 }
	5 16	10 20	219.1	Nason Creek	7.1	....	2 15	8 45
	5 34	10 27	222.1	Merritt	3.0	CK	2 08	8 30
	6 30	10 49	229.7	Berne	7.6	....	1 47	7 53
	{ 7 03 / 7 33 }	11 01	234.0	Cascade Tunnel	4.3	CO	1 34	7 33
	8 13	11 30	238.6	Cascade Summit	4.6	....	1 05	6 50
	9 03	12 21pm	245.9	Wellington	7.3	KA	12 21pm	{ 6 00 / 5 45 }
	9 59	12 53	255.3	Madison	9.4	MO	11 54	4 25
	{ 10 57 / 11 19 }	1 28	267.0	Skykomish	11.7	MS	11 19	{ 3 07 / 2 27 }
	11 50	1 50	274.8	Salmon	7.8	....	11 00	2 05
	12 16pm	2 06	281.3	Index	6.5	NX	10 45	1 39
	12 49	2 32	290.0	Gold Bar	8.7	....	10 26	1 04
	1 13	2 49	295.9	Sultan	5.9	UN	10 14	12 43
	1 42	3 12	303.2	Monroe	7.3	WA	9 58	12 15am
	2 11	3 35	310.5	Snohomish	7.3	S	9 40	11 46
	ar 2 41pm Daily	ar 3 55pm Daily	315.7	Lowell	5.2	K	lv 9 24am Daily	lv 11 14pm Daily
	ar 3 14pm	ar 4 21pm	321.2	Everett Junct	5.5	....	lv 9 10am	lv 10 40pm
	ar 6 12pm Daily	ar 5 47pm Daily	337.2	Seattle	36.0	X	lv 8 00am Daily	lv 7 40pm Daily

This first Great Northern Railway timetable took effect at 1:00 A.M. on Sunday, June 18, 1893. (Larry Lynde collection)

and dining cars trimmed in gold and polished oak and a library-observation car adorned Victorian-fashion with carpets, curtains, and wicker chairs. Accommodations also included a refreshment stand, a smoking room, indoor plumbing, and a barber shop, where businessmen could get a haircut and shave so they would be ready to attend a church social or city council meeting upon arrival at their destination.

A SHORTCUT THROUGH THE MOUNTAINS: THE FIRST CASCADE TUNNEL

In 1896, a profitable year for the railway, Hill gave orders to pursue building a tunnel under Stevens Pass to eliminate the troublesome switchbacks. Starting in 1897, it took three years with three shifts of men working seven days a week to complete the 2.6-mile-long tunnel. The story goes that while 800 men were working, 800 were sleeping, and 800 were standing at the bar.

Construction proved difficult to say the least. At the west end, the ground was so heavy with water that it took three concentric sets of support timbers to keep the tunnel from caving in. Completion of this tunnel was one of Great Northern's engineering feats. The survey proved so accurate that when the blasting crews met in the middle of the tunnel, having bored through from either end, the two sides were almost perfectly aligned.

Completion of the first Cascade Tunnel was cause for celebration: the expense of the trip was reduced and traffic delays because of heavy snowfall were lessened. But the tunnel created problems of its own. The long, narrow tunnel trapped the hot exhaust and smoke from the coal-fired engines. Train wheels slipped on soot-covered rails, slowing uphill trains and causing them to spend more time in the tunnel, making the problem worse. Temperatures climbed as high as 200°F in the locomotive cabs, and several crew members died from inhaling the carbon-monoxide-rich smoke.

In 1903 a train broke down inside the tunnel and the engine crew lost consciousness from smoke inhalation while trying to fix the problem. Most of the 103 passengers were also unconscious when an alert railway fireman riding as a passenger released the brakes and allowed the train to coast out of the tunnel to fresh air and safety.

Members of the press lambasted Hill for the tunnel's unsafe conditions. Finally, in 1909, the Great Northern electrified the tunnel to eliminate the hazardous exhaust. Electric locomotives pulled trains through the tunnel along 3 miles of trolley line. A dam and powerhouse in Tumwater Canyon generated power for the electric engines. The three-phase electrification system, which allowed the engines to use power when traveling uphill and generate power when going downhill, was the first and only such system in an American railroad tunnel.

CONTINUED DANGER

Although the electrified tunnel was a success, crossing the Cascades remained a daunting prospect. When first surveyed, the densely forested hillsides showed few signs of avalanches. That soon changed, however.

Logging, grade construction, and forest fires caused by sparks from passing trains created a barren landscape that made avalanches more likely, while the area's typically heavy snowfalls further increased the danger. Snow sometimes fell at a rate of 8 to 12 inches per hour and drifted as high as 75 feet.

To begin coping with the danger of avalanches, the railway built

This steam locomotive, built in 1908, has just loaded coal at Skykomish in preparation for crossing the Cascades. (Photo: Warren W. Wing collection)

eight snowsheds—the first in 1893, the year the first train rolled into Seattle. These early snowsheds were built with untreated 12-by-12-inch timbers, and some had 12-by-24-inch roof beams measuring as much as 42 feet long. Much of the wood was cut and milled locally from nearby stands of Douglas-fir, hemlock, and Pacific silver fir. The uphill snowshed wall consisted of timber cribbing that held back the earth and additional cribbing braced the downhill edge. More timbers created a sloped roof, which formed a continuous line with the mountainside so that any sliding snow would be carried downhill over the top of the tracks.

Snowsheds protected trains from sliding snow, but in many cases avalanches occurred where snowsheds were not yet in existence. In March 1910 an avalanche swept away two trains near Wellington, causing the largest fatal disaster in the history of the railway and closing the line for almost three weeks.

To restore the confidence of its passengers and curtail train delays, the Great Northern built more and longer snowsheds along the route. But these additional structures created new troubles, trapping smoke and hindering visibility. In addition, summer's heat caused the snowsheds to become tinder dry and vulnerable to sparks from passing trains.

With so many snowsheds along the line, annual maintenance soared. By 1910 many of the original wooden structures needed replacing, and heavy snows in the winter of 1912–13 crushed others. That year the railway hired 1,800 workers to make shed improvements along just 8 miles of track, and the need for additional sheds was clear.

In the winter of 1915–16, drifting snow and avalanches caused lengthy closures and fatalities. A slide collapsed a snowshed in December. Another buried three crew houses. In January of 1916, a series of slides on the Lower Grade destroyed a bridge and caused the line to be closed for a month. On the same day near Corea, a slide derailed a passenger train, killing eight and injuring twenty-two.

While making repairs on the Cascade Mountain snowsheds in 1917, the Great Northern Railway used over 35 million board feet of timber that cost triple what it had just eight years earlier. By this time, snowsheds and tunnels covered 6.7 of the 9 track miles between Wellington and Scenic.

Electric trains were first used to go through the First Cascade Tunnel. Their use was expanded and continued until they were replaced by diesels in 1956. (Photo: Warren W. Wing collection)

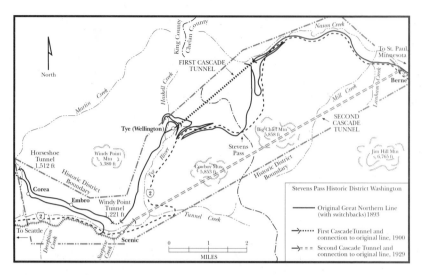

LOWER AND LONGER: THE SECOND CASCADE TUNNEL

In 1921 the Great Northern decided to abandon this trouble-some section of line and resurrected earlier plans for a longer, lower-elevation tunnel. Construction began in December of 1925 and continued at a record-breaking pace.

> *The construction took more than three years, cost $14 million, used 2,500 tons of dynamite and required 1,700 men at the height of activity. They lived in construction camps at Scenic on the west, Berne on the east, and at Mill Creek where there was a vertical shaft 622 feet deep about one-third of the way from the east end of the tunnel.*
>
> Wenatchee newspaper article

The Great Northern Railway dedicated the new 7.8-mile-long tunnel on January 12, 1929. By abandoning the first Cascade Tunnel and the grade between Berne and Scenic, they eliminated 6 miles of track, reduced the elevation by 502 feet, and avoided most of the snowsheds, thus cutting the expense of maintaining them.

In the words of a Great Northern official at the tunnel's opening ceremony, "the weakest link in our transportation chain has been replaced by one of the strongest." NBC Radio broadcast the opening ceremonies into the homes of millions of Americans, and President-elect Herbert Hoover spoke from Washington, D.C.—a reflection of the significance of the tunnel and of railroads to the nation.

The Great Northern's Legacy

The legacy of James J. Hill can be seen today in the giant container ships that visit the port of Seattle and unload their cargo onto the container trains that now pass below the Iron Goat Trail. It is a legacy that first began in 1896 when a ship from Tokyo docked in Seattle and unloaded its cargo of tea and spices onto a Great Northern train bound for East Coast and European markets via Stevens Pass.

Hill clearly understood the dual purpose of his transcontinental route. The first goal of the railroad was to provide a land bridge between Europe and Asia. In the process, and as a secondary effect, new markets for American commodities emerged along the route. Railway construction was paralleled by Hill's efforts to entice settlers to develop land and form irrigation programs, agricultural companies, and business centers such as Spokane, Wenatchee, Leavenworth, and Skykomish.

James J. Hill, "the Empire Builder," created his Great Northern Railway to serve as a transcontinental link between Europe and Asia, and open up new markets for American goods.

In Washington State, Hill won support for the Great Northern among leaders in the timber industry by offering free mill sites and low freight rates for timber. The timber giant, Frederick Weyerhaeuser, was one of those enticed to the Northwest through Hill's efforts.

In the *Story of the American Railroads*, historian Stewart Holbrook says of James J. Hill, "I can think of no other single American who had quite so much influence on quite so large a region." Hill died in 1916. He was seventy-eight years old.

Those Who Built the Great Northern

Both Hill's vision and his talented engineers were essential to Great Northern's success. But the railway wouldn't have been possible without the thousands of workers whose back-breaking labor turned the blueprints into smoothly operating lines.

When Chinese laborers became scarce, the Great Northern employed workers from Japan. This crew is working on the grade near Scenic. (Photo: University of Washington Libraries, Special Collections, Pickett 4176)

When workers laid the first rails across the Cascades, no roads existed in that rugged wilderness. Hauling tools on their backs, men built and maintained the line. Imagine this job during the winter of 1897–98 when 140 feet of snow fell in the area.

To build the first Cascade Tunnel, hardrock miners blasted through rock with hand tools and air compressor-powered drills. The monthly turnover among the 600-to-800-person construction crew averaged 300 to 400 men, a testament to the work's grueling nature.

The size and nature of the work force was determined not only by the Great Northern's construction and maintenance needs but by events far beyond Great Northern's control. For instance, the Chinese Exclusion Act of 1882 caused a sharp reduction in the availability of Chinese labor, which had been important in the construction of earlier western railroads. The Great Northern then turned to Japanese labor contractors who recruited workers from Japan and supervised their labor in exchange for a commission taken from each worker's pay.

Hard times in Europe also affected the work force. Census records from 1910 for Martin Creek/Skykomish show a population of diverse national origins: laborers came from Finland, Sweden, England, Canada, and Japan, and to a lesser extent, Germany, Norway, Scotland, Denmark, Austria, France, Russia, Italy, Switzerland, and China. They also came from within the United States, especially from New York, Illinois, Minnesota, Pennsylvania, and Iowa.

Recollections from these workers help us understand another side of history. The experiences of Japanese-American workers are better documented than most. Yoshiichi Tanaka, a worker on the Great Northern's Cascade Division from 1912 to around 1918, describes what his life was like:

> We laid new rails, changed ties, did leveling and adjusting, and took care of emergencies . . . even if it was midnight in the coldest part of winter, if there was an emergency we had to rush to the scene and make temporary repairs.
> . . . lodging facilities were awfully poor. Two rows of beds made of boards were run along the inside walls of old freight cars. Instead of mattresses, we spread straw on the boards . . . Innumerable bedbugs marched all over us . . .

Kazuo Ito,
ISSEI: A History of Japanese Immigrants in North America

THE TRAIL TODAY

As you walk the trail today, you will see remnants of the thirty-six years when this grade was a vital link in the railway line. Although the Great Northern abandoned this route over seventy years ago, many railway structures remain, challenging your imagination to complete the story. Compare what you see today with the historic photos in this guidebook and notice how trees and other plants have reclaimed the hillside where trains once came roaring past.

Remember to stay on the trail, out of tunnels, and off rotting timbers, which are prone to collapse. Staying on the trail will also protect the several species of rare grape-fern (*Botrychium*). These tiny ferns, found primarily in the Wellington area of the trail, are inconspicuous and very sensitive to trampling. Take nothing but pictures; leave nothing but footprints. By reducing your impact on this landscape and its historic features, you will make it possible for many others to enjoy the feeling of this place just as you have today.

James J. Hill once said, "Every person has a great adventure, the railway was mine." Join the thousands who walk along the Iron Goat Trail, explore its history, and make it your adventure too.

THE MARTIN CREEK TRAILHEAD

Trailhead, Parking Area, and Restrooms: Just up the road from today's trailhead, a unique engineering feat enabled Great Northern trains to travel up and down the mountain at a 2.2 percent grade. Eastbound trains coming up the Lower Grade passed through this area, crossed over Martin Creek, entered a horseshoe-shaped tunnel, and then crossed over Martin Creek again, this time on the Upper Grade. A train engineer just exiting the tunnel could look down the valley and see the rear of his train just entering the tunnel.

A family walking the Iron Goat Trail. (Photo: Mike Hall)

Debris slides have covered both ends of this tunnel. The abutments and footings are all that remain of the Martin Creek trestles.

The following section describes points of interest along the trail beginning at the Martin Creek Trailhead and heading east to Windy Point, which is halfway between the Martin Creek and Wellington Trailheads (see map on pages 36-37).

If you plan to start your hike at the Wellington Trailhead, turn to page 48.

> **Please note:** *The mile numbers assigned to the points of interest reflect the railroad's original mileage as measured from St. Paul, Minnesota. Today, milepost replicas have been installed along the trail, so it will be necessary for you to estimate the exact location of some points of interest based on their relationship to more obvious trail features. For example, the point of interest labeled 1717.5 is halfway between Mileposts 1717 and 1718.*

Hiking Options

Four different hikes are available from the Martin Creek Trailhead:

- *Option 1* is an easy 2.4-mile round-trip hike along the Lower Grade to the Twin Tunnels and back to the parking lot. This five-foot-wide trail is barrier-free, easy, level, and suitable for wheelchairs. It will be extended to Scenic in the future.
- *Option 2* is a moderate 1.4-mile round-trip loop hike along the Lower Grade, up the Martin Creek Crossover, east along the Upper Grade, down the Corea Crossover to the Lower Grade, and a right turn to go back to the parking lot.
- *Option 3* is a more difficult 6.1-mile round-trip hike along the Lower Grade, up the Martin Creek Crossover, east along the Upper Grade to Windy Point and back, down the Corea Crossover, and back to the parking lot.
- *Option 4* is a more difficult 6-mile one-way uphill hike from the Martin Creek Trailhead to the Wellington Trailhead. To make this hike, you need to arrange your own return transportation.

Points of Interest

All four hike options from the Martin Creek Trailhead begin at Milepost (MP) 1717.43.

Railway trestles and snowsheds stood at each end of the 170-degree horseshoe-shaped tunnel. The trestle in the foreground, built in 1900, was 160 feet high and 768 feet long. (Photo: University of Washington Libraries, Special Collections, Pickett 3961)

MP 1717.43 (Interpretive Kiosk)

The interpretive signs and map on the trailhead kiosk provide additional information about the Iron Goat Trail. Notice the trail follows both the Lower and Upper Railway Grade.

MP 1717.52 (Trail Register and Interpretive Sign)

Please stop and register the number of hikers in your party. Iron Goat Trail volunteers find it rewarding to know that thousands of people have already enjoyed this trail.

MP 1717.58 (Directional Sign)

Junction of Martin Creek Crossover and Lower Grade: This 0.11-mile spur trail connects the Lower Grade to the Upper Grade.

> *Option 1 hikers should continue east along the Lower Grade toward Twin Tunnels (see MP 1717.60 below).*

Option 2, 3, and 4 hikers should turn left here and hike up the Martin Creek Crossover (turn to page 31 and continue at MP 1717.58).

MP 1717.60 (Interpretive Sign)

Snowshed Benches: This rocky slope between the Upper and Lower Grades is all that remains of a snowshed's rock foundation.

The first step in snowshed construction was building a timber cribbing to hold back the earth. Later, more cribbing was added to brace the downhill edge, and the wooden roof was sloped in a continuous line with the mountainside.

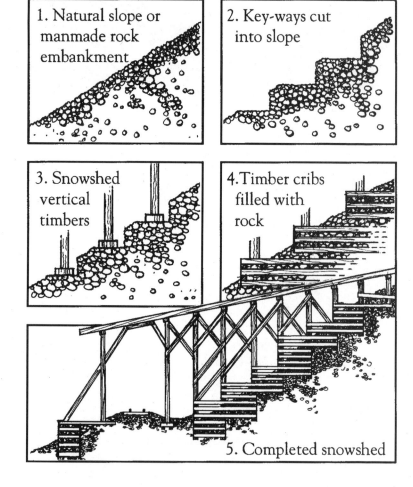

1. Natural slope or manmade rock embankment

2. Key-ways cut into slope

3. Snowshed vertical timbers

4. Timber cribs filled with rock

5. Completed snowshed

Snowsheds covered the tracks and protected the trains from snow and rock slides.

MP 1717.77 (Interpretive Sign)

Where Corea Once Stood: This level, relatively unwooded area once held a depot and structures that housed workers.

Nearby, archaeologists found fragments of ceramic bowls used by Japanese workers. They also found remnants of two rock and brick domed ovens, the type used by Italian and possibly other ethnic railway workers to bake bread. You can see a domed oven by visiting the "Bygone Byways" interpretive trail (see Appendix 3: Nearby Places of Interest).

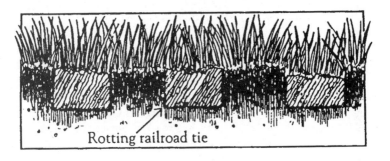

Rotting railroad tie

MP 1717.86

Corrugation: As you walk along this section of trail, watch for any open grassy areas on your right. You may notice that the moss-covered ground has a corrugated surface. The depressions were made by railway ties left behind to rot in place. ***Please stay on the trail so that others can see this in the future.***

MP 1717.91 (Viewpoint, Bench, and Interpretive Sign)

Men who worked on maintenance and snowshed construction during the summer often shoveled snow in winter. Camps were established along the line to feed and house hundreds of workers.

While working in this area, volunteers found fuki (pronounced foo-kee) plants, a Japanese variety of coltsfoot, which are apparently descended from root stock brought here and planted by laborers.

MP 1717.94 (Directional Sign)

Junction of Corea Crossover and Lower Grade: This 0.33-mile spur trail connects the Lower Grade with the Upper Grade. In railroad terms, a "crossover" is a connection from one railroad track to another. This crossover was built recently for trail hiking and did not exist during the railroad era.

Please continue on the Lower Grade.

MP 1718

This milepost, re-created in the style of those used by Great Northern, shows that you are 1,718 rail miles from St. Paul, Minnesota, the railway's headquarters, as measured along the original route over the summit of Stevens Pass.

MP 1718.32 (Viewpoint and Interpretive Sign)

From here you can hear and see U.S. Highway 2 in the distance, and, if you time it right, a train may rumble by. Listen carefully; you can tell from the sound whether a train is traveling up or down grade.

It's hard to imagine, but photos from the turn of the century show us that many of these hills were logged or burned by fires started by sparks from trains; a dreary picture compared to the beautiful mountains of green we see today.

As you can see from this view, however, the railroad continues to influence the land. In August 1992, sparks from a rail grinder, used to smooth the rails, set fire to the nearby brush. The fire, called the Big Grinder Fire, quickly spread uphill, burning 257 acres of forest before fire fighters stopped the blaze close to the boundary of the Alpine Lakes Wilderness.

MP 1718.36 (Bench and Interpretive Sign)

Rock Cut: Notice the looming rock faces on each side of the trail. Great Northern workers used dynamite to blast a cut through this rock outcropping. James J. Hill and his crews were determined to punch this line to the Pacific Coast.

MP 1718.51 (Interpretive Signs)

Twin Tunnels: Railway workers built this tunnel and its nearby twin in 1916 after a harsh winter crushed the bridge that originally covered this expanse. The Twin Tunnels were among the many improvements made to the line that summer. The east portal of this tunnel and the second of the Twin Tunnels are not visible from this section of trail.

In front of the tunnel, you will see a 96-foot concrete arch which served as a permanent snowshed, directing sliding snow and debris over the tracks. Drains within the arch carry away seeping water that would otherwise build up pressure behind the wall. The arch was built wide enough for two tracks because the Great Northern had always planned to widen the tunnel from one track to two. The remains of the wooden snowshed cribbing you see today were part of the snowshed connecting the concrete arch and the tunnel.

Stay out of the tunnel. Rotting timbers and falling rock make it unsafe.

MP 1718.56 (Viewpoint and Interpretive Sign)

Troubling avalanches and debris slides didn't leave with the railway. In 1990 a torrent of water, trees, rocks, and mud roared down this hillside, damaging the Upper Grade above you, this section of the Lower Grade, and some Forest Service and county roads farther down the hill.

This debris flow marks the end of the maintained trail. Volunteers for Outdoor Washington expect to extend this trail 1.5 miles to a future trailhead and parking lot at Scenic, along U.S. Highway 2.

This completes the points of interest for Hike Option 1. To return to your vehicle, turn around and follow the same trail back to the Martin Creek Trailhead parking lot.

Option 2, 3, and 4 hikers continue on. See MP 1717.58 below.

MP 1717.58 (Directional Sign)

Junction of Martin Creek Crossover and the Lower Grade: Hike up the Martin Creek Crossover to the Upper Grade. A bench and an interpretive sign are located halfway up this trail. During railway construction and later salvage operations, Great Northern workers hauled materials along this crossover between the Upper and Lower Grades.

MP 1716.40 (Directional Sign)

Junction of Martin Creek Crossover and the Upper Grade: From here, the original grade continued west into the brush where trains would cross over Martin Creek, enter the Horseshoe Tunnel, and turn onto the Lower Grade. Milepost 1717 lies within the collapsed tunnel.

Turn right and follow the trail east along the Upper Grade.

MP 1716.36 (Interpretive Sign)

Snowshed Cribbing: Here you can see what's left of the rock-filled timber cribbing, which retained the earth and stabilized the up-hill side of a snowshed. The remains of many railway structures still exist along the trail. Use your imagination and see if you can figure out what they were. Rusty sheets of metal could have been a water flume; a pile of timbers and concrete footings, the remains of a snowshed.

For your safety, do not climb on rotten timbers.

MP 1716.25 (Viewpoint and Interpretive Sign)

If you were hiking this grade in 1913, you would be under the cover of a snowshed here on the Upper Grade, looking down onto the roof of another snowshed that protected the Lower Grade.

MP 1716.14 (Spur Trail to Tunnel and Interpretive Sign)

Tunnel #14: This tunnel, constructed in 1892, was the only tunnel used when the Great Northern first crossed the Cascades in 1893. As its name implies, it was the fourteenth tunnel on the original route from St. Paul to Seattle. A timber snowshed once abutted this tunnel and protected the track from snow and sliding debris. The other end of the tunnel has collapsed.

The trail follows the temporary construction route used by Great Northern trains while this 312-foot tunnel was being built.

MP 1716

This milepost, re-created in the style of those used by the Great Northern, shows that you are now 1,716 miles from St. Paul, Minnesota, the railway's headquarters, as measured along the original route over the summit of Stevens Pass.

MP 1715.99 (Directional Sign)

Junction of Corea Crossover and the Upper Grade: This 0.33-mile spur trail connects the Upper Grade with the Lower Grade. In railroad terms, a "crossover" is a connection from one railroad track to another. This crossover was built recently for trail hiking and did not exist during the railroad era.

> *Option 2 hikers should turn right and follow the Corea Crossover down to the Lower Grade (see MP 1717.94 below). A bench and an interpretive sign are located halfway down this switchback trail.*

Option 3 and 4 hikers should continue east along the Upper Grade (turn to page 34 and continue at MP 1715.99).

MP 1717.94 (Directional Sign)

Junction of Corea Crossover and the Lower Grade: Turn right and follow the trail toward the parking lot. (If you turn to the left the trail leads to the Twin Tunnels, adding a 1.3-mile round-trip to your hike; turn to MP 1718 on page 30.)

MP 1717.91 (Viewpoint, Bench, and Interpretive Sign)

Men who worked on maintenance and snowshed construction during the summer often shoveled snow in winter. Camps were established along the line to feed and house hundreds of workers.

While working in this area, volunteers found several fuki (pronounced foo-kee) plants, a Japanese variety of coltsfoot, which are apparently descended from root stock brought here and planted by laborers.

MP 1717.86

Corrugation: As you walk along this section of trail, watch for any open grassy areas on your left. You may notice that the moss-covered ground has a corrugated surface. The depressions were made by railway ties left behind to rot in place. ***Please stay on the trail so that others can see this in the future.***

MP 1717.77 (Interpretive Sign)

Where Corea Once Stood: This level, relatively unwooded area once held a depot and structures that housed workers.

Nearby, archaeologists found fragments of ceramic bowls used by Japanese workers. They also found remnants of two rock and brick domed ovens, the type used by Italian and possibly other ethnic railway workers to bake bread. You can see a domed oven by visiting the "Bygone Byways" interpretive trail (see Appendix 3: Nearby Places of Interest).

MP 1717.60 (Interpretive Sign)

Snowshed Benches: This rocky slope between the Upper and Lower Grades is all that remains of a timber snowshed's rock foundation.

This completes the points of interest for Hike Option 2. To return to your vehicle, continue on the Lower Grade past the Martin Creek Crossover to the trailhead parking lot.

HIKE OPTIONS 3 AND 4

MP 1715.99 (Directional Sign)

Junction of the Corea Crossover and the Upper Grade: Continue east following the Upper Grade.

MP 1715.36

Stream Washout: After crossing a series of small streams, you will cross a large stream in an avalanche-prone area. In 1990 a torrent of water, trees, rocks, and mud roared down this hill at 20 to 50 miles per hour. The debris flow washed out this section of the Upper Grade, portions of the Lower Grade, Forest Service Road 6710, and the Old Cascade Highway, leaving this jumble of rocks. Today, slide alder thrives in this site.

MP 1715.21

Rock/Crib Wall: Here the trail splits into two parallel trails. Take the stone steps to the lower walkway. To your left is a rock wall that supported the railway grade. Culverts were installed in the rock wall to channel water underneath the grade where it would slowly dissipate. On your right are the remains of timber cribbing that supported the downhill side of a snowshed. The snowshed kept debris out of this drainage system.

Volunteers first found this rock trench filled with impenetrable vegetation—big enough to trap an elephant. They nicknamed it "The Elephant Trap." Only after this section of trail was cleared did they understand its true purpose.

MP 1715.08

West End, Snowshed Wall 1715.08: As winter weather continued to damage the original wooden snowsheds and the cost of timber rose, the Great Northern Railway turned to a combination concrete-and-timber snowshed design for more stability. The walls that you see along this trail are the backwalls of these snowsheds; missing on each are the wooden roof and vertical front wall on the downhill side.

If you look near the stream at the west end of this wall, you will see some timber cribbing: a clue as to how these massive walls were built.

This snowshed wall was built in 1917 and is 518 feet long. Notice the weep holes every 10 feet along the wall. These weep holes relieve water pressure by allowing water to pass through the wall and into the concrete gutter. The fact that these drainage features are still working in spite of over seventy years of abandonment is a testimony to the skills of the Great Northern Railway engineers.

MP 1715

You are now 1,715 rail miles from St. Paul. If you had traveled here by a Great Northern passenger train in 1893, it would have taken you approximately two and a half days, assuming no delays. Compare this journey to a five-month trip by wagon train in the mid-1800s.

MP 1714.97 (Staircase and Interpretive Sign)

Spillway Spur Trail: This 500-foot spur trail leads you to a spillway and reservoir built in the hillside above this snowshed wall. Snowsheds

Construction of a combination concrete and timber snowshed by the Great Northern Railway. By 1917, snowsheds and tunnels covered 6.7 of the nine track miles between Wellington and Scenic. (Photo: George Fischer collection)

Iron Goat Trail

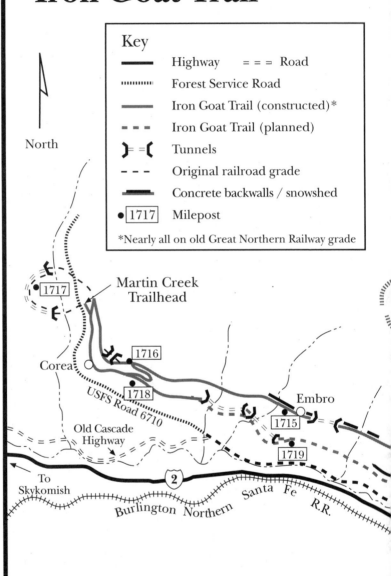

Key

———— Highway = = = Road

·············· Forest Service Road

———— Iron Goat Trail (constructed)*

- - - Iron Goat Trail (planned)

)= =(Tunnels

- - - Original railroad grade

▬▬▬▬ Concrete backwalls / snowshed

●⬜1717 Milepost

*Nearly all on old Great Northern Railway grade

North

1717

Martin Creek
Trailhead

1716

Corea

1718

USFS Road 6710

Embro

1715

Old Cascade
Highway

1719

To
Skykomish

2

Burlington Northern Santa Fe R.R.

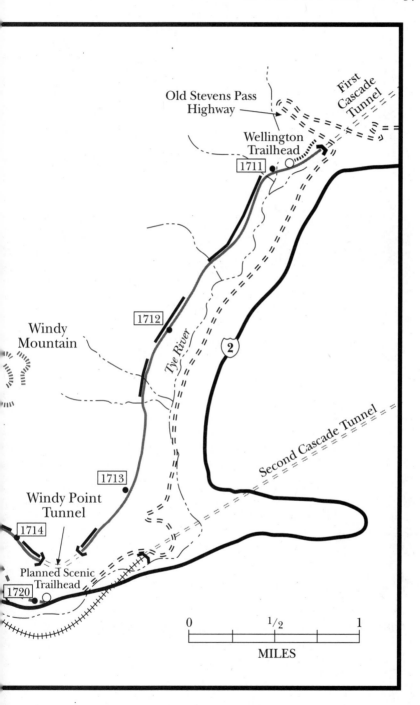

The depot at Alvin, later renamed Embro, was protected by a snowshed. (Photo: J. D. Wheeler, from the George Fischer collection)

became tinder dry in summer and were at risk of catching fire from the sparks of passing trains. To address the fire hazard, the Great Northern developed two water systems: one system was located in Wellington; the other system was fed from this reservoir.

Reservoir water was funneled in wire-wound wooden pipes and gravity-fed to snowsheds along the line. At approximately every 200 feet along a timber snowshed there was a galvanized iron standpipe. These standpipes, or fire hydrants, were connected to fire hoses on the inside of the snowshed and on the roof. This spillway and fire system was originally designed and built in 1910, then reconstructed in 1914.

MP 1714.93

Embro: This site housed a telegraph station and workers' shacks. It was first known as Alvin but renamed Embro in 1914. Steam-powered trains stopped here for water in order to continue the 2.2 percent grade climb up the mountain toward Wellington.

Please remember that any artifacts you find along this trail have historical significance and should be left on the site for others to enjoy.

MP 1714.80

West End, Wall 1714.80: This wall is 193 feet long and was the backwall of a combination (concrete and timber), double-track-width snowshed built in 1916. It replaced an earlier all-timber snowshed in need of repairs.

MP 1714.77 (Spur Trail to Tunnel and Interpretive Sign)

West Portal, Embro Tunnel: Notice the piles of rocks on the downhill side of the grade. These were extracted in 1916 during construction of this 462-foot-long timber-lined tunnel. Tunnels were often lined with timber to protect trains from rock fall caused by freezing and thawing.

MP 1714.67

East Portal, Embro Tunnel; West End, Wall 1714.67: When you go around the Embro Tunnel, you will see a 39-foot-long concrete archway. This was built in 1916 as a permanent snowshed to protect trains from falling debris. A cheaper and less permanent combination snowshed was then built adjacent to the arch in 1916. The concrete backwall that remains is 475 feet long.

As you continue your hike toward Windy Point you will pass three more concrete backwalls, making it easy to understand where these snowsheds once stood. But the railway also built all-timber snowsheds between each of these more permanent combination concrete-and-timber designs. If you had walked along this track in 1917, you would have walked the entire distance between here and Windy Point—almost a mile—under the cover of some type of snowshed.

MP 1714.50

West End, Wall 1714.50: This combination snowshed was built in 1916 and is 225 feet long.

MP 1714.22

West End, Wall 1714.22: This combination snowshed was built in 1916 and is 540 feet long. Notice the concrete footings in the trail tread. These footings braced the vertical timbers which supported the roof structure.

MP 1714.16

Fallen Flume: These 12-by-12-inch timbers were lined with sheet

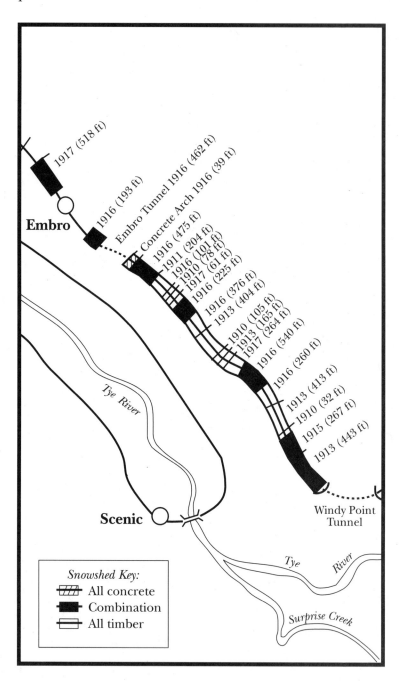

Snowsheds between Embro and Windy Point.

In 1913, the west portal of the Windy Point Tunnel was under construction, designed for a single track. The following year the tunnel was enlarged to the width of a double track, but the second track never became necessary. (Photo: Great Northern Railway Archives)

metal and used as a flume to channel stream water. The timber roof of this combination snowshed once supported this flume and the water was routed across the roof and over the edge.

MP 1714

This replica of a Great Northern milepost indicates you are 1,714 railroad miles from St. Paul, Minnesota.

MP 1713.99

West End, Wall 1713.99: This snowshed wall was built in two parts: the western section was built in 1915, and the eastern section was built in 1913, for a total length of 710 feet. This snowshed butted up against the west portal of Windy Point Tunnel.

MP 1713.85 (Interpretive Sign)

West Portal, Windy Point Tunnel: This tunnel was originally built in 1913 for a single track. It was enlarged in 1914 to the width of a double track, although the railway never found it necessary to lay the second track.

Because the tunnel is unsafe, the trail follows the original grade used by trains prior to 1913. Imagine yourself on a train as it rounds this sharp curve while clinging to the mountainside.

MP 1713.60 (Viewpoint and Interpretive Sign)

Windy Point Viewpoint: From the top of this rock outcrop, you can see the present-day railroad tracks in the valley below as they enter the 7.8-mile-long second Cascade Tunnel. Trains pass through that tunnel approximately twenty times a day, so if you're lucky, a

In 1913, the west portal of the Windy Point Tunnel was under construction, designed for a single track. The following year the tunnel was enlarged to the width of a double track, but the second track never became necessary. (Photo: Great Northern Railway Archives)

train may pass by or you may see smoke from a recent train puffing from the tunnel's portal.

This completes the points of interest for Hike Option 3 from the Martin Creek Trailhead to Windy Point. Windy Point is halfway between the Martin Creek and Wellington Trailheads.

To see the east portal of the Windy Point Tunnel before returning to the Martin Creek Trailhead, follow the trail around the corner, onto the two-foot-wide ledge of the concrete arch, and go down the steps to the portal. To return to the Martin Creek Trailhead, turn around and follow the Upper Grade back to its junction with the Corea Crossover. At this point turn to MP 1715.99 on page 32, rejoin Hike Option 2, and follow the points of interest down the Corea Crossover, along the Lower Grade, and back to the parking lot.

Option 4 hikers should continue on this trail toward Wellington (turn to page 56 and follow the interest points backward from Windy Point [MP 1713.60] to the Wellington Trailhead).

THE STORY OF WELLINGTON

Nearly 1000 feet above the noise and activity of the mainline lies the silent remains of a town named Wellington. Like any other ghost town there are spirits hovering in the air at Wellington. Let your imagination wander and let these ghosts come alive. The roar of the Tye River can become another eastbound freight pulling into the yard. Is it the rustle of the autumn wind, or is it the sound of traction blowers on a passing GE electric? In the midst of the gloom and solitude of the concrete shed, is it just the natural silence of this remote area, or is it the tragic silence that settled on this rail town in the wee hours of March 1, 1910?

Martin Burwash, *Cascade Division*

Wellington was a small mountain town that lived and died to serve the railway. From 1893 to 1929 Wellington was the operational headquarters for tunnel construction, tunnel electrification, and general maintenance along the line. It was also a vital coal, water, and rest stop for

Wellington was an active railroad town from 1893 to 1929. This photograph, taken looking east, shows the Bailets Hotel (left behind the runaway track), the depot (center near the mainline), and the coal tower, power plant, and Haskell Creek bridge footings (on the right side of the tracks). (Photo: Washington State Historical Society, Tacoma, Curtis and Miller photo, #27094)

trains heading over the Cascades. Life in Wellington was like that of any other town, a place where people came and went; buildings and houses were built, torn down, or moved to different locations. Life was sometimes joyful, sometimes difficult for the many who called this place home. The Bailets Hotel—which housed a general store, post office, dining room, tavern, and card room—a workers' bunkhouse and several cabins, a train depot, coal chute, engine house, water tank, and, for a while, a school served as the primary structures in Wellington.

As trains came and went, life carried on. Stories are told of kids who traded fish for free train rides to their favorite fishing hole. Workers traveled from miles around for a social function or church service in Wellington. Many also remember the town's great fire in 1926. It spread rapidly through Wellington's covered walkways and burned many houses before townspeople dynamited the walkways, stopping the fire just shy of the school.

Avalanche!

Although the town of Wellington existed for thirty-six years, only one event put its name on the map: the avalanche of 1910. The following is a brief account of the eight days leading up to the disaster when over one hundred people were detained in trains on this snowy mountainside.

My Dear Husband and Children:

I with a hundred or so are snowbound here. We got in at eleven Tuesday the 22nd. We stayed east of Cascade Tunnel until Thursday the 24th when they got us as far as Wellington. After we got away the building in which we took our meals collapsed and killed two men. Yesterday it turned to raining and they thought surely we would get out but today it snowed hard all day. . . . We can hardly see the top of the mountains; they are so high . . . We get good meals at a house two blocks away [Bailets Hotel]. I am trusting in God to save us.

Mrs. Sarah Jane Covington wrote this letter as her passenger train and a mail train were parked on the passing tracks along the outside edge of Wellington Yard. As the storm continued, hillsides of snow, trees, and rocks continually slid over the tracks around Windy Point west of Wellington. Rotary snowplows worked at a feverish pace, but a low coal supply and the immensity of the slides made the task nearly impossible.

Such a snow you never saw. It's banked up to the top of the window here and we can't go or come. Can't get any information as to when we'll get out . . . . Have been reading and smoking all day long . . .

This letter by Ned Topping was written
on Great Northern Railway stationery

By Saturday, food rations limited the passengers to two meals a day. With no sleep and little pay, snow shovelers quit working. The rotary plows were out of coal, and all communication wires had come down in the storm.

We had a [church] service on the cars . . . we got two meals today, a lady borrowed a phonograph and we had some music but people are getting very blue.

Mrs. Sarah Jane Covington

Mysterious roars filled the silence, the sound of avalanches coming down the surrounding mountains. Restless passengers demanded the train be moved back into the tunnel, but Superintendent O'Neill assured them of their safety.

Perched on the side of a mountain now –a wooded hill to my right and deep valley on other side.

Ned Topping

Passengers were fed up with the wait, and on Monday, February 28, a few braved the treacherous hike over the slides and down a dangerous avalanche chute to Scenic.

Monday night—still in this snow—if nothing happens I expect to leave in the morning for Scenic—down the track for 2 or 3 miles then down the side of the mountain. There are numbers of people going so I'll have company. Oh if I ever get out of this place how happy I will be and if nothing happens I'll be free tomorrow.

Ned Topping

Early in the morning of Tuesday, March 1, an avalanche swept down the mountainside, striking the trains and pitching them into the gulch below, leaving only the end of one coach and some rotary blades visible. The "Wellington Avalanche" just missed Bailets Hotel

The Wellington Avalanche of March 1, 1910, hit the west end of town, just missing the Bailets Hotel and the train depot, but striking numerous snowbound train cars. (Photo: Lee Pickett, from the Jerrold F. Hilton collection, courtesy of George Fischer)

and the train depot, but fifteen train cars, coaches, a half dozen locomotives, engines, and sheds were buried.

Wellington residents immediately started searching for survivors. A worker hiked the tracks to Windy Point and down to Scenic to report the disaster. A relief train from Everett brought doctors, nurses, coroners, undertakers, sheriffs, and detectives as far as Scenic. From there they struggled a thousand feet uphill through the deep snow to the disaster site. By the time they arrived, all those still alive had been found.

In the midst of thunder, lightning, and falling snow, rescue workers hauled victims out of the gulch. The motorman's bunkhouse became a makeshift hospital; the freight shed became the morgue. It took until March 7 for rescuers to locate the last of the wreckage and to transport bodies by sled down the chute to Scenic.

Ned Topping, a thirty-eight-year-old salesman from Ashland, Ohio, wrote in his letter each day until he died in the avalanche. The letter was found in his clothing. Mrs. Sarah Jane Covington was returning to Seattle to meet her husband for their golden anniversary. Her letter was found in her handbag amongst the wreckage.

The railroad tracks from Scenic were finally cleared on March 12, enabling the remaining bodies to be removed from Wellington by train. After the spring snowmelt revealed the last body, ninety-six people were known to be dead.

(For further information on the Wellington Avalanche, see Selected Readings at the back of this book.)

THE WELLINGTON TRAILHEAD

Trailhead, Parking Area, and Restrooms: Imagine yourself on a train pulling into Wellington in the early 1900s. For the most part, the hillsides would show scars of fires or logging. The town would be laid out in the flat area to the north, and you would see Bailets Hotel, some cabins, and the school, connected to other buildings by covered walkways.

On the hills to the north, east, and south, you would be able to see five switchback tracks where trains traveled out to a spur, stopped, switched tracks, and continued with the opposite end of the train in the lead.

Fifteen train cars, coaches, a half-dozen locomotives, engines, and sheds were buried by the 1910 disaster. (Photo: J. D. Wheeler, from the Warren W. Wing collection)

Before 1900, Great Northern trains climbed four levels of gradual switchbacks to cross Stevens Pass. The passenger train shown on level three is approximately where U.S. Highway 2 runs today. (Photo: George Fischer collection)

It took three ten-wheeled engines to move a seven-car passenger train over the switchbacks—two locomotives on the front end and one backed against the last car, allowing reverse movements on the switchbacks. The locomotive engineers coordinated movements using a system of whistles.

The following section describes points of interest along the trail beginning at the Wellington Trailhead and heading west to Windy Point, which is located halfway between the Wellington and Martin Creek Trailheads (see map on pages 36-37).

> ***Please note:*** *The mile numbers assigned to the points of interest reflect the railroad's original mileage as measured from St. Paul, Minnesota. Today milepost replicas have been installed along the trail, so it will be necessary for you to estimate the exact location of some points of interest based on their relationship to more obvious trail features. For example, the point of interest labeled 1717.5 is halfway between Mileposts 1717 and 1718.*

Hiking Options

Four different hikes are available from the Wellington Trailhead:

- *Option 1* is an easy one-half mile round-trip hike to the west portal of the first Cascade Tunnel and back to the parking lot. This 5-foot-wide trail is barrier-free and suitable for wheelchairs.
- *Option 2* is an easy one-half mile round-trip hike to the site of the Wellington Avalanche and uphill back to the parking lot. This 5-foot-wide trail is barrier-free and suitable for wheelchairs.
- *Option 3* is a more difficult 6-mile round-trip hike downhill at a 2.2 percent grade to the Windy Point Tunnel and uphill back to the parking lot. This minimum 3-foot-wide trail is barrier-free and suitable for wheelchairs (at a moderate level) to the east portal of the tunnel.
- *Option 4* is a more difficult 6-mile, one-way downhill hike from the Wellington Trailhead at a 2.2 percent grade to the Martin Creek Trailhead. To make this hike, you need to arrange your own return transportation.

Points of Interest

All four hike options begin from the Wellington Trailhead, Milepost (MP) 1710.92.

MP1710.92 (Interpretive Kiosk)

The interpretive signs and map on the trailhead kiosk provide additional information about the Iron Goat Trail. From the parking lot and trailhead, a barrier-free trail leads east toward the first Cascade Tunnel and west toward the all-concrete snowshed. This is the original grade of the Great Northern Railway.

MP 1710.88 (Interpretive Sign Located on Island in Parking Lot)

Tye Depot: The depot was relocated to this site after the all-concrete snowshed was built. The original station was named Wellington, like the town, but after the avalanche of 1910, passengers didn't want to travel through the infamous town of Wellington, so the railway changed the name of the station to Tye. Mail was still delivered by the Post Office to the town of "Wellington."

> *Option 1 hikers should travel east along the trail to the west portal of the first Cascade Tunnel. Begin at MP 1710.88 below.*

Option 2, 3, and 4 hikers should travel west along the trail toward Windy Point (turn to page 52 and continue at MP 1710.93).

MP 1710.88 (Interpretive Sign)

Coal Tower Footings: The original coal tower was damaged in the 1910 avalanche. These footings were part of the new coal tower rebuilt in this location. The footings are now exposed because of excavations in the area; however, the tops of the footings were originally at ground level.

MP 1710.84 (Interpretive Sign)

Rotary House and Motorshed Footings: The 300-foot-long electric engine house was used to service electric motors and rotary plows. The original building was destroyed in the 1910 avalanche and was rebuilt the following year at this location.

MP 1710.70 (Interpretive Sign)

Water Tank: The trail leads you between the footings for a 100,000-gallon water tank, which supplied water for steam locomotives and fire protection along the line. Snowsheds became tinder dry in summer and were at risk of catching fire from the sparks of passing trains. To address the fire hazard, the Great Northern developed gravity-fed water systems like this one in Wellington.

MP 1710.69 (Interpretive Signs)

West Portal, First Cascade Tunnel: From 1893 to 1900, the railway used a series of switchbacks to traverse Stevens Pass and come down into the town of Wellington. After this 2.6-mile-long first Cascade Tunnel was complete, the switchbacks were abandoned. From 1900 to 1929, trains traveled from Cascade Station on the east side of the pass through this tunnel and into Wellington.

The tunnel is 16 feet wide with a 2-foot-thick concrete lining, and it is 21 feet from the top of the rail to the arch in the roof. The tracks are on a 1.7 percent grade downhill from Cascade Station to Wellington.

This completes the points of interest for Hike Option 1. To return to your vehicle, turn around and follow the same trail back to the Wellington Trailhead parking lot.

Great Northern locomotive No. 2512 emerging from the west portal of the First Cascade Tunnel on August 10, 1924. (Photo: James A. Turner, from the Warren W. Wing collection)

HIKE OPTIONS 2, 3, AND 4

MP 1710.93 (Interpretive Sign)

Power Plant Footings: From the top of this concrete wall, it is difficult to imagine yourself in the steam power plant, which hung over the edge of the bank. Coal was delivered to the top level and gravity fed to the boiler on the lower level. Steam heating pipes then ran underground to various railway buildings such as the beanery (dining hall) and depot.

MP 1710.97 (Interpretive Sign)

Haskell Creek Bridge: Located here are the original bridge footings and wing walls for the railroad bridge across Haskell Creek.

Originally, the rushing river could be seen through the open plank-
ing of this bridge. In later years the railway channeled the creek
into a culvert and filled in the area to the level you see today.
Haskell Creek (named for Charles F. B. Haskell, who scouted
Stevens Pass for the original right-of-way), runs into the Tye River
(W. H. Tye was a Great Northern engineer) and then into the
Skykomish River.

MP 1710.98 (Interpretive Sign)
Runaway Track: Do you see the slope of the runaway track? An
out-of-control train would gain speed coming downhill through the
tunnel and across the Wellington Yard. This 1,800-foot-long runaway
track was used to stop these trains before they continued down the
mountain.

MP 1711
This milepost is a replica of the Great Northern mileposts. Rail
miles were measured from St. Paul, Minnesota, the railway's headquarters. They included the original mileage across the mountain
switchbacks.

MP 1711.02
Original Wellington Depot: Built on this location in 1893, the
Wellington Depot faced west toward the hillside, greeting trains
as they came into the backside of town via the switchbacks. When
the 2.6-mile-long first Cascade Tunnel was completed in 1900, the
depot was turned around to face this new railway grade. In late
1910 the Great Northern Railway made plans to build the all-
concrete snowshed, so the depot was moved east and renamed
Tye. The site of the Tye Depot is located at the east end of the parking
lot island.

MP 1711.04 (Interpretive Sign)
East End, All-Concrete Snowshed: During the summers of 1910
and 1911, Great Northern spent approximately $680,000 to con-
struct this 2,462-foot-long permanent snowshed. The railway also
removed, relocated, or reconstructed several railway buildings
that were either damaged in the avalanche or were standing on
this site. Originally designed to protect Great Northern trains, this
snowshed has become a lasting memorial to those who died in the
Wellington Avalanche.

MP 1711.30 (Spur Trail and Interpretive Signs)

This is the site of the 1910 Wellington Avalanche. Three interpretive signs tell the story.

This completes the points of interest for Hike Option 2. To return to your vehicle, turn around and follow the same trail back to the Wellington Trailhead parking lot.

> *Option 3 and 4 hikers should continue on the trail toward Windy Point. See MP 1711.54 below.*

MP 1711.54 (Interpretive Sign)

East End, Wall 1711.54: As harsh winters continued to weaken the original wooden snowsheds and the cost of timber rose, the Great Northern Railway turned to a combination concrete backwall and wooden snowshed design. This new type of snowshed provided more stability than all-timber structures but was not as expensive as the all-concrete design. The concrete walls that you see along this trail are the backwalls of these snowsheds; missing on each are the wooden roof and vertical front wall on the downhill side. If you had walked on this track in 1917, you would have been under the cover of either an all-timber or combination snowshed for almost the entire distance between here and Windy Point.

After abandoning this route, the Great Northern salvaged many of the rails, ties, and snowshed timbers for use elsewhere on the line. However, many railway structures remain, challenging your imagination to fill in the story. Rusty sheets of metal could have been a water flume; a pile of timbers and concrete footings, the remains of a timber snowshed.

Please remember that any artifacts you find along this trail have historical significance and should be left in place for others to enjoy.

MP 1711.87

East End, Wall 1711.87: Built in two stages in 1913 and in 1915, this combination snowshed has a total length of 1,433 feet. Two methods were used in its construction. Where the slope of the excavation was steep and rocky, a concrete wall was built and fixed into the rock with a reinforced concrete anchor. More often, however, a concrete wall was built using rubble to weight its base and gravity to hold the wall in place.

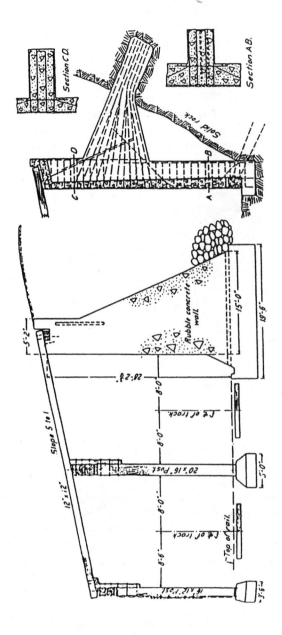

Concrete backwalls of combination snowsheds were either built using rubble and gravity to hold the wall in place or walls were fixed to rock with a reinforced concrete anchor. (Railway Age Gazette, April 17, 1914)

MP 1711.80 (Interpretive Sign)
Rotary Plow and Crew

MP 1712.27
East End, Wall 1712.27: This combination snowshed was first built in 1913 and extended in 1915 and 1916 to reach its current length of 1,532 feet. The front walls of snowsheds were designed with shutters that were closed in winter but removed during warm months, allowing smoky exhaust to escape and providing visitors with a view.

MP 1712.57 (Interpretive Sign)
Collapsed Snowshed: **Please stay off the snowshed, rotting timbers may collapse.**

MP 1713
At this point you are 1,713 track miles from St. Paul, Minnesota. If you had traveled here from St. Paul by a Great Northern passenger train in 1893, it would have taken you approximately two and a half days, assuming no delays.

MP 1713.41
East End, Wall 1713.41: This double-track combination snowshed was 737 feet long and was built in two parts between 1914 and 1915. It butted against the east portal archway of the Windy Point Tunnel.

MP 1713.55 (Interpretive Sign)
East Portal, Windy Point Tunnel **(end of barrier-free trail)***:* As you stand in this portal, you are looking at the 288-foot concrete archway built in 1914 when the tunnel was expanded to a double-track width. It served as a permanent snowshed to protect the train and tracks from falling rock outside the tunnel entrance.

Because it is dangerous to enter the tunnel, the trail follows the original right-of-way used by trains to travel around Windy Mountain before the tunnel was built. Go up the steps and follow the trail along the two-foot-wide footings of the concrete arch along the outside of the tunnel, and around a rock outcropping.

MP 1713.60 (Viewpoint and Interpretive Sign)
Windy Point Viewpoint: From the top of this rock outcrop, you can see the present-day railroad tracks in the valley below as they enter the 7.8-mile-long second Cascade Tunnel. Trains pass through this

tunnel approximately twenty times a day, so if you're lucky, a train may pass by or you may see smoke from a recent train puff from the tunnel's portal.

In contrast to the first Cascade Tunnel, the second Cascade Tunnel has an effective, efficient ventilating system. Fans clear the air completely within 25 minutes after the passage of a diesel-powered train. Troubles from coal exhaust are a thing of the past.

Just beyond the west portal of Windy Point Tunnel is the avalanche chute that rescue workers climbed to retrieve the victims of the Wellington Avalanche. Imagine the scene as they struggled through the drifting snow, following the grade around this steep cliff. When the rescue workers returned they lowered the bodies by rope down to the trains waiting at Scenic.

This completes the points of interest for Hike Option 3 from Wellington to Windy Point. Windy Point is halfway between the Wellington and Martin Creek Trailheads. If you would like to return to the Wellington Trailhead, turn around and follow this trail back to the parking lot.

Option 4 hikers should continue west on the trail toward the Martin Creek Trailhead (turn to page 42 and follow the interest points backward from Windy Point [MP 1713.60] to the Martin Creek Trailhead via the Corea Crossover Trail and the Lower Grade).

 # The Trail Tomorrow

The USDA Forest Service and Volunteers for Outdoor Washington continue to work together to extend the Iron Goat Trail (IGT). Help is always needed for trail construction and maintenance. To donate labor, materials, or money, contact the following:

Volunteers for Outdoor Washington (VOW)
8511 15th Avenue Northeast, Room 206
Seattle, WA 98115-3199
(206) 517-4469
VOW Website: www.volunteer-outdoors.org
IGT Website: www.bcc.ctc.edu/cpsha/irongoat
IGT information line (206) 283-1440

Skykomish Ranger District
P.O. Box 305
Skykomish, WA 98288
(360) 677-2414 or (425) 744-3260

Mount Baker–Snoqualmie National Forest
21905 64th Avenue West
Mountlake Terrace, WA 98043-2278
Website: www.fs.fed.us/r6/mbs

Lake Wenatchee Ranger District
(509) 763-3103

Outdoor Recreation Information Center
(206) 470-4060

If you have additional questions or wish to report harmful activity along the trail, please contact one of the organizations listed above.

A scenic view along the Iron Goat Trail. (Photo: Ruth Ittner)

Appendix 1:
Plants Found Along
the Iron Goat Trail

This list of plants is only a small sample of the more than 220 species which have been found in this area by Washington Native Plant Society members.

Evergreen Trees
Douglas-fir *(Pseudotsuga menziesii)*
Mountain hemlock *(Tsuga mertensiana)*
Western hemlock *(Tsuga heterophylla)*
Noble fir *(Abies procera)*
Pacific silver fir *(Abies amabilis)*
Western or Pacific yew *(Taxus brevifolia)*
Western redcedar *(Thuja plicata)*

Deciduous Trees
Black cottonwood *(Populus trichocarpa)*
Red alder *(Alnus rubra)*
Sitka alder *(Alnus sinuata)*
Big-leaf maple *(Acer macrophyllum)*
Douglas maple *(Acer douglasii)*
Vine maple *(Acer circinatum)*

Shrubs
Cascade Oregon grape *(Berberis nervosa)*
Devil's club *(Oplopanax horridum)*
Five-leaved bramble, Strawberry bramble *(Rubus pedatus)*
Kinnikinnick, Bearberry *(Arctostaphylos uva-ursi)*
Oregon boxwood, Mountain-lover *(Pachistima myrsinites)*
Red elderberry *(Sambucus racemosa)*
Red-flowering currant *(Ribes sanguineum)*

A Great Northern aster blooms alongside the trail. (Photo: Ruth Ittner)

Red huckleberry *(Vaccinium parvifolium)*
Salal *(Gultheria shallon)*
Salmonberry *(Rubus spectabilis)*
Twinflower *(Linnaea borealis)* (sub-shrub)

HERBACEOUS PLANTS

Star-Flowered Solomon's Seal

Aster family (Asteraceae)

Coltsfoot *(Petasites frigidus* var *palmatus)*
Great Northern aster *(Aster modestus)*
Indian thistle, Edible thistle *(Cirsium edule)*
Lily family *(Liliaceae)*
Bronze bells, Western stenanthium *(Stenanthium occidentale)*
Clasping-leaved twisted-stalk *(Streptopus amplexifolius)*
Columbia lily *(Lilium columbianum)*
Oregon fairy-bells *(Disporum hookeri)*
Star-flowered Solomon's seal *(Smilacina stellata)*
Western trillium *(Trillium ovatum)*

Orchid family (Orchidaceae)

Calypso, fairy slipper *(Calypso bulbosa)*
Coral-root, spotted *(Corallorhiza maculata)*
Rattlesnake-plantain *(Goodyera oblongifolia)*

Other plants in miscellaneous families

Cascade penstemon *(Penstemon serrulatus)*
Cow-parsnip *(Heracleum lanatum)*
Foamflower *(Tiarella trifoliata)*
Fringecup *(Tellima grandiflorum)*
Hedge-nettle *(Stachys cooleyae)*
Monkey-flower, yellow *(Mimulus guttatus)*
Pacific bleedingheart *(Dicentra formosa)*
Pig-a-back, thousand mothers *(Tolmiea menziesii)*
Siberian miner's lettuce *(Montia sibirica)*
Sitka columbine *(Aquilegia formosa)*
Skunk cabbage *(Lysichitun americanum)*
Stinging nettle *(Urtica dioica)*
Violet, evergreen *(Viola sempervirens)*
Violet, stream or pioneer *(Viola glabella)*
Wild ginger *(Asarum caudatum)*

FERNS

Bracken *(Pteridium aquilinum)*
Deer-fern *(Blechnum spicant)*
Lady-fern *(Athyrium filix-femina)*
Leathery grape-fern *(Botrychium multifidum)*
Licorice-fern *(Polypodium glycyrrhiza)*
Maidenhair spleenwort *(Asplenium trichomanes)*
Northern maidenhair *(Adiantum pedatum)*
Parsley-fern *(Cryptogramma crispa)*
Sword-fern *(Polystichum munitum)*
Virginia grape-fern *(Botrychium virginianum)*

Wild Ginger

APPENDIX 2:
BIRDS FOUND ALONG
THE IRON GOAT TRAIL

These birds are those most likely to be seen while walking on the trail. Many others may be heard or occasionally seen. This list was provided by members of the Seattle Audubon Society.

Blue grouse
Barred owl
Rufous hummingbird
Downy woodpecker
Hairy woodpecker
Pileated woodpecker
Olive-sided flycatcher
Western wood-pewee
Pacific-slope flycatcher
Steller's jay
Common raven
Black-capped chickadee
Chestnut-backed chickadee
Red-breasted nuthatch
Brown creeper
Winter wren
Golden-crowned kinglet
Swainson's thrush
Hermit thrush
American robin
Varied thrush
Warbling vireo
Black-throated gray warbler
Townsend's warbler
Wilson's warbler
Western tanager
Dark-eyed junco

Downy Woodpecker

Blue Grouse

APPENDIX 3:
NEARBY PLACES
OF INTEREST

The area adjacent to the Iron Goat Trail is rich in recreational and interpretive opportunities including:

- *Skykomish* served as a division point for the Great Northern Railway. On Railroad Avenue you will see many historic buildings. A brochure for a self-guided walking tour is available.
- *Deception Falls picnic area and nature trail* is located at Milepost 56.7 on U.S. Highway 2. The kiosk displays interpretive signs relating to the Great Northern Railway and Stevens Pass Historic District. A picnic shelter and restrooms are available.
- *Stevens Pass Ski Area* at the summit of Stevens Pass includes multiple chair lifts plus three day lodges and other amenities.
- *Trails for hiking, cross-country skiing, or snowshoeing* are numerous. For over a mile, the Pacific Crest National Scenic Trail follows the original grade of the Great Northern Railway. This section of track over Stevens Pass was used by the railway from 1893 to 1900.
- *Mill Creek Nordic Ski Area* is located east of Stevens Pass on U.S. Highway 2.
- *Bygone Byways* is a short railroad history interpretive trail east of Stevens Pass on U.S. Highway 2.
- *Tumwater Dam*, completed in 1909, provided power for electric locomotives traveling through the first Cascade Tunnel and later the entire route between Skykomish and Wenatchee. In 1956 the railroad converted to diesel and closed the Tumwater Hydroelectric Project. The dam, with an interpretive sign, still stands in Tumwater Canyon.
- *Leavenworth* used to be a division point for the Great Northern Railway, where the change of crews took place. Today it has been transformed into a tourist mecca with a Bavarian theme.

 # SELECTED READINGS

HISTORY

Anderson, Eva. *Rails Across the Cascades*. Wenatchee, Wash.:World Publishing Co., 1952.

Burwash, Martin. *Cascade Division*. Arvada, Colo.: Fox Publications, 1995.

Burwash, Martin. *The Great Adventure, The Railroad Legacy of Stevens Pass*. Arvada, Colo.: Fox Publications, 1995.

Great Northern Railway Historical Society Magazine. Reference Sheets 172, 175, 179,183, 213.

Haskell, Daniel C., ed. *On Reconnaissance for the Great Northern: Letters of C. F. B. Haskell, 1889-1891*. New York: New York Public Library, 1948.

Hidy, Ralph W., and Muriel E. Hidy, et al. *The Great Northern Railway, A History*. Boston, Mass.: Harvard Business School Press, 1988.

Hult, Ruby El. *Northwest Disaster*. Portland, Ore.: Binfords and Mort, 1960.

Ito, Kazuo. *ISSEI: A History of Japanese Immigrants in North America*. Seattle, Wash.: Executive Committee for Publication, Japanese Community Service, 1973. English and Japanese language editions.

Moody, Don. *America's Worst Train Disaster: The 1920 Wellington Tragedy*. Plano, Tex.: Abique, 1998.

Roe, JoAnn. *Stevens Pass: The Story of Railroading and Recreation in the North Cascades*. Seattle, Wash.: The Mountaineers, 1995.

Wood, Charles R., and Dorothy Wood. *The Great Northern Railway: A Pictorial Study*. Edmonds, Wash.: Pacific Fast Mail, 1979.

BOTANY

Hitchcock, C. L., and A. Cronquist. *Flora of the Pacific Northwest*. Seattle, Wash.: University of Washington Press, 1973.

Pojar, James, and Andrew MacKinnon. *Plants of the Pacific Northwest Coast*. Vancouver, B.C.: Lone Pine Publishing, 1994.

Taylor, Ron. *Mountain Plants of the Pacific Northwest*. Missoula, Mont.: Mountain Press Publishing Co., 1995.

WHO FINANCED THE IRON GOAT TRAIL?

The construction and interpretation of the Iron Goat Trail requires a rather remarkable team effort. Volunteers for Outdoor Washington and Mount Baker–Snoqualmie National Forest are grateful to all the organizations involved in generously supporting the project with dollars, in-kind contributions, and/or participation. They are:

Recreation and Conservation Groups—
- Alpine Lakes Protection Society
- The Mountaineeers
- The Mountaineers Foundation
- Rails to Trails Conservancy
- Sierra Club, Cascade Chapter
- Stevens Pass Greenway
- Stevens Pass Ski Club
- Washington Native Plant Society
- Washington Trails Association.

Historical Agencies and Organizations—
- Association of King County Historical Organizations
- Center for Puget Sound History and Archaeology, Bellevue Community College
- Great Northern Railway Historical Society
- Kettle Valley Steam Railway, British Columbia
- King County Landmarks and Heritage Commission Hotel-Motel Tax Fund
- League of Snohomish County Historical Associations
- Museum of History and Industry, Seattle
- North Central Museum, Wenatchee
- Northwest Railroad Museum
- Pacific Northwest Historians Guild
- Skykomish Historical Society

- Snohomish County Community Heritage Program
- Washington State Heritage Corridors Program
- Washington State Heritage Caucus
- Washington State Historical Society.

Institutions of Higher Education and Professional Societies—
- American Public Works Association, Washington Chapter
- American Society of Civil Engineers, Seattle Section
- Pacific Lutheran University, Anthropology Department
- Project Management Institute
- Seattle University, Department of Civil and Environmental Engineering
- University of Washington, College of Forest Resources.

Federal, State and Local Government—
- USDA Forest Service
- Washington State Interagency Committee for Outdoor Recreation
- Capital Projects Fund for Washington's Heritage
- Washington State Legislature
- Washington State Parks and Recreation Commission
- Washington State Department of Transportation
- King County Arts and Heritage Initiative
- King County Department of Parks and Recreation
- King County Department of Transportation
- Snohomish County Parks and Recreation Division
- Town of Skykomish

Private Sector—
- Alpine Rockeries, Inc.
- Bradbury Press
- Burlington Northern Santa Fe
- Cadman Sand and Gravel
- Dunn Lumber Company
- Everett Steel Mills, Inc.
- Great Northern Railway Cascade Division Reunion
- Northwest Bolt and Nut
- Osberg Family Trust
- Palmer G. Lewis, Inc.
- Phoebe W. Haas Charitable Trust
- The William Penn Foundation
- Puget Sound Energy

- Pyramid Communications
- Seattle Film Works
- Seattle Works (formerly The Benefit Gang)
- Shannon and Wilson, Inc.
- Spicers Paper, Inc.
- Stevens Pass, Inc.
- Tacoma Screw Products
- 3 Worlds Studios
- Tree Top, Inc.
- Washington Coalition of Citizens with DisABILITIES

In addition hundreds of individuals, through financial contributions and volunteer effort, have contributed to the construction, maintenance, and interpretation of the Iron Goat Trail.

Volunteers for Outdoor Washington

Volunteers for Outdoor Washington (VOW) was founded as a nonprofit organization in 1982 "to promote volunteer stewardship of natural, heritage, and outdoor recreation resources in partnership with land management agencies."

VOW volunteers contribute about 20,000 hours annually in natural resource maintenance projects in Western Washington. Among VOW's high profile projects are the Iron Goat Trail and the Robe Canyon Historic Park. VOW has earned a reputation for providing high-quality training for other organizations that want to participate in the citizen effort to maintain trails. The training motto is "be safe, have fun, and perform work that meets professional standards." VOW has been a leader in promoting collaboration among organizations representing trail users of all types.

THE MOUNTAINEERS, founded in 1906, is a nonprofit outdoor activity and conservation club, whose mission is "to explore, study, preserve, and enjoy the natural beauty of the outdoors{4ell}" Based in Seattle, Washington, the club is now the third-largest such organization in the United States, with 15,000 members and five branches throughout Washington State.

The Mountaineers sponsors both classes and year-round outdoor activities in the Pacific Northwest, which include hiking, mountain climbing, ski-touring, snowshoeing, bicycling, camping, kayaking and canoeing, nature study, sailing, and adventure travel. The club's conservation division supports environmental causes through educational activities, sponsoring legislation, and presenting informational programs. All club activities are led by skilled, experienced volunteers, who are dedicated to promoting safe and responsible enjoyment and preservation of the outdoors.

If you would like to participate in these organized outdoor activities or the club's programs, consider a membership in The Mountaineers. For information and an application, write or call The Mountaineers, Club Headquarters, 300 Third Avenue West, Seattle, Washington 98119; (206) 284-6310.

The Mountaineers Books, an active, nonprofit publishing program of the club, produces guidebooks, instructional texts, historical works, natural history guides, and works on environmental conservation. All books produced by The Mountaineers are aimed at fulfilling the club's mission.

Send or call for our catalog of more than 300 outdoor titles:

The Mountaineers Books
1001 SW Klickitat Way, Suite 201
Seattle, WA 98134
1-800-553-4453
e-mail: mbooks@mountaineers.org
website: www.mountaineersbooks.org

OTHER TITLES YOU MAY ENJOY FROM THE MOUNTAINEERS:

100 CLASSIC HIKES IN WASHINGTON, *Ira Spring & Harvey Manning*
A full-color guide to Washington's finest trails by the respected authors of more than thirty Washington guides, written with a conservation ethic and a sense of humor, and featuring the best hikes in the state.

WASHINGTON STATE PARKS: A Complete Recreation Guide, Second Ed., *Marge & Ted Mueller*
Well-known, thorough, and reliable guide to all of Washington's state parks, detailing four-season activities in nearly 200 state recreation areas.

100 HIKES IN™ WASHINGTON'S SOUTH CASCADES AND OLYMPICS: Chinook Pass, White Pass, Goat Rocks, Mount St. Helens, Mount Adams, Third Ed., *Ira Spring & Harvey Manning*
Our best-selling hiking guide to this region, newly revised and featuring new color photos, with thoroughly researched, succinct hike descriptions by the area's most respected hiking gurus.

HIKING THE GREAT NORTHWEST: The 55 Greatest Trails in Washington, Oregon, Idaho, Montana, Wyoming, British Columbia, Canadian Rockies, and Northern California, Second Ed., *Ira Spring, Harvey Manning, & Vicky Spring*
The latest edition of this classic hiking guide to the most spectacular trails in the region, featuring new color photos and the personal picks of a trail-tested team of Northwest hiking gurus.

A WATERFALL LOVER'S GUIDE TO THE PACIFIC NORTHWEST: Where to Find Hundreds of Spectacular Waterfalls in Washington, Oregon, and Idaho, Third Ed., *Greg Plumb*
The complete, newly revised guide to more than 500 Pacific Northwest waterfalls accessible by foot, car, and boat, with fifty new waterfalls described and rated for aesthetic value.

BEST HIKES WITH CHILDREN, IN WESTERN WASHINGTON AND THE CASCADES, Volumes 1 & 2, Second Eds., *Joan Burton*
Thoroughly revised editions of the top-selling books in the *Best Hikes with Children,* series, featuring new hikes appropriate for families, seniors, and anyone who enjoys an easy dayhike.

AN OUTDOOR FAMILY GUIDE TO WASHINGTON'S NATIONAL PARKS: Mount Rainier, Mount St. Helens, North Cascades, The Olympics, *Vicky Spring & Tom Kirkendall*
A three-season guide to the best selection of outdoor activities in Washington's spectacular national parks, with information on flora and fauna, history, safety, and tips on successful outdoor outings with children.

SEATTLE'S LAKES, BAYS & WATERWAYS: AFOOT & AFLOAT Including the Eastside, *Marge & Ted Mueller*
The newest in the popular *Afoot & Afloat* series, featuring city escapes for boaters and shoreside explorers.

WASHINGTON'S BACKCOUNTRY ACCESS GUIDE: National Parks, National Forests, Wilderness Areas, *Ken Lans*
Completely updated compilation of Washington backcountry information from a variety of sources, highlighting recent regulation changes and featuring the latest access, trail conditions, and permit information.

ACCESSIBLE TRAILS IN WASHINGTON'S BACKCOUNTRY: A Guide to 85 Outings, *The Washington Trails Association.*
Everything you need to know, from trail grade and surface to guidelines for safety, and much more.

Outdoor Books by the Experts

Whatever the season, whatever your sport, The Mountaineers Books has the resources for you. Our FREE CATALOG includes over 350 titles on climbing, hiking, mountain biking, paddling, backcountry skiing, snowshoeing, adventure travel, natural history, mountaineering history, and conservation, plus dozens of how-to books to sharpen your outdoor skills.

All of our titles can be found at or ordered through your local bookstore or outdoor store. Just mail in this card or call us at 1·800·553·4453 for your free catalog.

Name _____
Address _____
City _____ State _____ Zip+4 _____ - _____
E-mail _____

Please send another catalog to my friend at:
Name _____
Address _____
City _____ State _____ Zip+4 _____ - _____
E-mail _____

624-3

Attention Western Washington residents:

Wanna go outside and play?

Join The Mountaineers today!

You may think we're just a climbing club but The Mountaineers offer a lot more. We sponsor regular outings and classes on hiking, backcountry skiing, backpacking, alpine scrambling, bicycling, first aid, photography, sailing, sea kayaking, trail maintenance, and conservation. There are activities for families, singles, and active people of all ages. Other benefits of joining The Mountaineers include the use of four terrific mountain lodges and the opportunity to join our exotic foreign excursions. And, of course, we offer hundreds of climbs each year for all levels of experience.

If you live in Western Washington, there's a Mountaineers Club near you. To receive membership information, just mail in this card today!

300 Third Avenue West
Seattle, WA 98119
206·284·6310
www.mountaineers.org

Name _____
Address _____
City _____ State _____ Zip+4 _____ - _____
E-mail _____

624-3

BUSINESS REPLY MAIL

FIRST-CLASS MAIL   PERMIT NO. 85063   SEATTLE, WA

POSTAGE WILL BE PAID BY ADDRESSEE

THE MOUNTAINEERS BOOKS
1001 SW KLICKITAT WAY STE 201
SEATTLE WA 98134-9937

BUSINESS REPLY MAIL

FIRST-CLASS MAIL   PERMIT NO. 75491   SEATTLE, WA

POSTAGE WILL BE PAID BY ADDRESSEE

THE MOUNTAINEERS
300 3rd AVE W
SEATTLE WA 98119-9914